S0-BDQ-339

Earline Irwin

ONE-TRICK PONY

God's Simple Plan to Save the World

Phillip E. Long

Copyright © 2005 by Phillip E. Long

One-Trick Pony
by Phillip E. Long

Printed in the United States of America

ISBN 1-59781-706-6

All rights reserved solely by the author. The author guarantees all contents are original and do not infringe upon the legal rights of any other person or work. No part of this book may be reproduced in any form without the permission of the author. The views expressed in this book are not necessarily those of the publisher.

Scripture taken from the New American Standard Bible ®, Copyright © 1960, 1962, 1963,1968, 1971, 1972, 1973, 1975, 1977, 1995 by The Lockman Foundation. Used by permission.

www.xulonpress.com

For

Phillip Jacob, Dirk Evan, Simon Andrew, & Jena Marie

~ In case you ever wondered what I really thought ~

~ CONTENTS ~

Acknowledgments

Gratitude is a thing, like many others, which can easily exceed language. Lists of names rarely capture its immensity. It must pass through persons, but is only satisfied when it finally finds it's home with God.

To my family, who have endured my stumbling efforts to live what I write; To my friends, who have encouragingly shown interest in my effort; To the stranger, who told me that I could write and then became a friend who taught me how; To those who's lives have given me endless examples of the love of God—incarnate again; Thanks for a taste of the new wine.

Preface

Too many people have rejected the good news of Jesus Christ without ever even understanding what they've missed. It makes me wonder if that should really be counted as rejection. I mean to ignore a misconception or caricature of Jesus, as presented by some earnest or bumbling believer, can't honestly be called a rejection of Jesus Himself. It might actually be a sign of honesty and integrity on the part of a skeptical listener. If the message received includes no answer for the deepest longings of the human soul, why should it be accepted as the final word from God?

God has guaranteed that those who seek Him will find Him, when they seek with their whole heart. It follows then, that when they find Him they will know that they have— with their whole heart.

No, the final Word from God is Jesus Christ. Any cheap substitute that merely satisfies our own need for affirmation, desire for success, or for a workable philosophical model will never adequately convey the Truth of God. We can commit all kinds of errors in our effort to tell the story but, for the story to have any ultimate meaning, it must be true. The truth about God is that, apparently, He loves us—and gave His Only Son as a sacrifice to redeem us. If we don't make God's love clear, then we haven't told the truth. And if we aren't telling the truth, why should anyone believe us anyway?

For many believers, sharing the gospel with others is like telling a joke poorly. So poorly in fact, that the audience doesn't get the joke. Making a valiant attempt to explain the joke further only renders it less funny with every explanation. The words are all there and everyone gets it, but the humor is gone for good.

I'm not trying to say that the Good News of Jesus Christ is a joke, or even that it's funny. Only that if it were, there aren't enough skilled comedians among us to make people laugh. It's too bad, because people need to laugh and humor relies on timing and delivery.

Conveying the gospel is very much about timing and delivery too. Sometimes the best way to learn how to tell a joke is to be around funny people. Spend time with the guy who always has people in stitches. Copy his delivery and mimic his timing. Explaining jokes more thoroughly is not going get you a gig. Making people laugh will.

Another thing is for certain. It's really hard to tell a joke you don't understand yourself. If it didn't make you laugh; it probably isn't going to come across that well when you pass it along. That's why good comedians are the ones who always seem to be laughing about something. They see life differently than the rest of us—then they help us see it.

Love is the humor in the gospel. It often gets lost among all the good explanations. Sharing the gospel without communicating God's love is like telling a great joke—and blowing the punch line.

One-Trick Pony: a.) American slang phrase indicating a person who relies on a single skill or ability in every situation. b.) A small horse that is capable of doing only one trick.

1

Why Bother?

Who in Their Right Mind Would Read This?

"...so that men would seek Him and perhaps reach out for Him and find Him, though He is not far from each one of us." (Acts 17:27)

There once was a boy who believed in God. On the day his father was murdered, he decided to start over. The things he believed about God no longer made any sense to him. God was either different than he had always thought or God wasn't there at all.

As it turns out, God was different than he thought.

God is different than most people think.

The boy began to wonder about all he had learned and began to ask questions. He had lots of questions. In answer, he was given empty words about God that satisfied neither his mind nor his heart. He resolved to never again accept empty words and call them his own.

He listened to sincere people who believed that their opinion regarding the identity of Jesus was the entire basis of their hope—though they read in their Bibles that Satan is of the same opinion.

He observed people who saw nothing amiss as they arranged good deeds for someone they actually despised. He was dismayed by those who were so sure they had God figured out they didn't even notice how hypocritical they had become.

But most of all, he was sorry about all of the good questions that never got asked and he was sorry for the people who never bothered to ask them.

As he grew older, he learned that certainty was rarely a reliable path to truth. Humility worked so much better. He discovered that unless you had already arrived at truth, certainty only prevents you from ever getting there. At least that was true of the kind of certainty that looked so much like pride or fear.

He also noticed that many Christians were content to believe that the "Good News" about Jesus Christ means only that the Old Covenant is satisfied. With the final sacrifice offered and the debt for sin paid, they appeared unconcerned with the New Covenant spoken of by the prophet Jeremiah. They seemed indifferent to God's promise to write His law in their minds and upon their hearts. It seemed to the boy that they had stopped just short of becoming.

More time went by. As the young man matured, he considered what it would be like if God's law was written on his own heart. He wondered how God might go about writing it there. He noticed people who appeared to have God's law written on their hearts. He decided that he wanted to be like them.

He decided that he wanted God to write on his heart and so he tried very hard to make it happen.

As it turns out, God is the One who makes it happen.

I am that young man, and eventually I became a father. I now have children of my own and want God to write on their hearts too. I want them to believe in God.

It is for their sake that I have committed my thoughts on faith and Christian living to paper for general consumption and certain criticism. Perhaps the reader should exercise a measure of caution. I do not hold any degrees in formal Christian education. I have founded no famous Christian ministries. I am not a leader, a theologian, or a celebrity. Few, outside of my family and close friends, seek my advice or counsel on any subject of great and lasting truth or relevance.

I suppose that I am a lot like most of the people who might bother to read this short book. I have no theological credentials that permit me to critique or make definitive statements about the direction or practice of Christianity.

I realize, of course, that an airline pilot with an unremarkable vocabulary might have little of substance to add to any discussion about walking with God and discovering truth and meaning in life. But then, neither might a fisherman, tax collector, or carpenter. These questions might best be reserved for highly educated professionals.

After all, Christian faith, scripture, and doctrine are inexhaustible sources of knowledge and understanding about the infinite, eternal God Himself. To accept my simple contribution might be seen as reducing the essence of God's great plan to mere childlike faith and simplicity.

So who am I?

I'm 47 years old and have been involved in aviation most of my adult life—as a military pilot and a commercial pilot. I married my high school sweetheart and we have four children.

I've been unemployed and restarted my career. I've buried people I love. I've rented apartments and built homes. I operate heavy machinery and write poetry. I sing my own lyrics and hunt wild game, but neither very well. I am frequently wrong, occasionally right, and cautiously impulsive.

I've been a Christian since I was seven and have doubted, questioned, and trusted God relentlessly for nearly forty years. I have, in this life, outlived my father and, quite possibly, figured out my mother. I have loved deeply, hoped freely, and been both rewarded and wounded for the effort. I have lived my faith, and observed others living their faith, in God. I've asked myself some hard questions and found some satisfying answers. Some of the conclusions I've made are troubling and some are thrilling.

As a pilot, I'm mostly concerned with what works; what will get me to my destination safely. I am also concerned with the possibility of drifting off course. I understand that, without a compass oriented to true north and instruments correctly aligned to keep the blue side up, I could fly right into the ground or into a mountain in the darkness or the fog. The result is that I'm not easily impressed by "Sunday School" answers that are often repeated with great conviction but little comprehension as to how they might apply to a world full of people and airplanes that need to get somewhere.

I believe in the God of the Bible. I don't claim to know exactly what He is up to most of the time.

I believe that God loves me. I doubt that means He is obligated to please me.

I believe God desires us to reflect His image within us as we live our lives. I believe that we can.

I believe that "The Word became flesh and dwelt among us." I believe the Spirit of God continues to become flesh today, in the church, when we let Him.

I believe Jesus Christ is the Word of God and the Only Begotten Son of God. I don't know quite how to explain that clearly and simply without being labeled a heretic.

I believe God promises eternal life for those who love Him. I don't presume that it includes this body I now inhabit.

The title of this book captures my understanding about God, Jesus Christ, and Christianity perfectly. It amuses me that this is a phrase normally used in contempt or derision. That somehow seems fitting. I, however, intend it in the most complimentary way possible.

I have come to view Jesus Christ as a "One-Trick Pony" of sorts. His one and only "trick" is sacrificial love. But what a trick it is! It is the revelation of God Himself. It is the plan of God...the power of God...the purpose of God. It is His work and our witness. It is His will and our pleasure.

It is what He has written on the hearts of His children and is the source of the obedience of faith. It is the fulfillment of His law.

It is the very best apologetic in the world and the finest curriculum for Christ-like growth ever suggested. It takes everything into account and reveals the wisdom and character of God for every situation. I have come to believe that

Christians are called to such a faith in God that they too become one-trick ponies. They become just as He was in the world so that others will be drawn to Him.

In fact, I believe we were designed for such a life and can only find it and our true selves when the piece of us that won't have anything to do with it has died. When we lose our life for His sake, we find it. Until then, we merely theorize and speculate.

I have written this series of stories and essays to guide my children along the path I have explored. My goal is not to convince them of a particular viewpoint, but rather to paint a picture with stories so vivid that it reminds them of something they've always imagined, and it takes their breath away.

If I can show them how a few pieces of the puzzle go together, they might begin to see the picture for themselves. But it would be good to remember that these are stories. Stories have a way of telling the truth without being obvious. So be careful, this is not systematic theology.

If I achieve my goal with this small book, many of the ideas you have at the end of the journey will be your own. Only then will you discover if they are of lasting value.

May God's Spirit engage your heart and mind to love Him fully and become more and more like His very own Son, Jesus Christ.

2

Treasure Hunt

If We Have What We Want, Why Do We Search?

"The Kingdom of Heaven is like a treasure hidden in the field, which a man found..." (Matthew 13:44)

H o Chi Min Trail, North Viet Nam, 1967. My dad, the father of six children at the time, flies his Grumman OV-1 Mohawk at low altitude with the infrared radar on. He maintains total radio communication silence. His airplane is blacked out. He takes pictures. He's looking for something.

Back in Kansas, we children are looking for something too.

Mother, raising six children with Daddy away in a war from which he may not return, has a lot on her mind. From time to time, she needs a break. To get one this day she hands us a small piece of paper with a short cryptic clue written on it.

She tells us, "If you follow the clue and any others you might find along the way, there's a treasure waiting for you...somewhere." In a farmhouse you call the "Pink Palace" on a big acre surrounded by orchards, fields, and gardens somewhere could be anywhere.

To find a treasure, clues will be needed.

We unfold the clue and the oldest reads, "High above the place where eggs are made."

Piece of cake. Every morning someone feeds the chickens and collects the eggs. The only place "high above" would have to be on top of the chicken coop. Those of us who could scramble, scramble to the place where eggs are made. After all, we know there is a treasure.

On the roof of the chicken coop, we find a second note. It says, "Nobody ever checks the mousetraps."

For a brief instant, we all think perhaps one of us is in trouble for not doing his chores properly. But soon we remember that this is a game and there are several mouse-traps in the old Pink Palace. We'll have to split up to save time checking them all for clues.

All morning long we tear around—inside, outside, upside, downside—hunting, like a funny little band of crazed monkeys, and searching for a precious "buried trea-sure". Probably candy. Some clues are easy. Some are incredibly hard and emissaries have to be dispatched to Mother for hints so the quest can resume.

These games could go on for hours, yet to us treasure hunters that time stood still.

You had to be there when we found the treasure. The excitement was a living thing that possessed us all. The frenzy of desire for treasure overwhelmed us. We wanted it.

We knew one thing for sure: when you find a treasure, nothing else matters.

So, the question you might want to ask is this one: What else matters? Because, when you find a treasure, nothing else matters.

Of course, you know when you've found a treasure. It's not something you wonder about. You don't just sit there and think, "Hmm... is this a treasure? Hmm... it could be... I think... hmmm."

No. You know.

Likewise, you definitely know when you haven't found a treasure. It's obvious from the fact that you're still looking. If you observe the people you know well, you quickly see that most of them haven't found a treasure yet. So much still matters.

Now everyone who was ever a child knows, deep down inside, that there really is a buried treasure somewhere. Even if they don't say it out loud so all the neighbors and relatives hear about it, they still keep looking. And they are still as sure as a child that when they find it, nothing else will matter.

Sometimes at night, when no one else is paying attention, the treasure hunters dig around in the dark. They look in the malls and department stores too. They look at Wal-Mart and Home Depot, even at work and on their vacations. They look at church and on camping trips to the wilderness. On the Internet, they search the world. They check eBay and chat rooms, weblogs and news links, even behind pop-up ads and in spam.

There has to be a treasure out there, because everyone seems to be looking for it. You know it must still be there...somewhere.

It's odd, but if you think about it for long you realize it's true. The places everybody keeps checking have already been checked before. The people who checked Home Depot are still looking. The people who checked the wilderness are still looking. So are all the ones who checked on the cruise ships and beaches and ski resorts and Mount Everest, even the bottom of the Indian Ocean. They are all still looking for the treasure. Some even get stuck looking in the same place over and over and over.

And since they're still looking, there must still be a treasure.

Of course, we all know someone who has decided that nothing else matters and then jumped off the deep end. It's easy to be confused about what matters. "Nothing else matters" means that, in comparison, everything else truly *is* insignificant.

Not everyone whose life is consumed by a single thing has found the treasure. Not a cocaine junkie who desperately needs another fix or a power hungry dictator who murders innocent people for control. Not an addict to some twisted perversion who just can't escape or a thieving corporate CEO who will do anything for more money.

A treasure isn't like that. A treasure is good. It's precious. That's why it's called a treasure and that's why nothing else matters.

It's more like a drink of water when you're lost in the desert and you've run out.

It's like a breath of fresh air when you're under water and can't get to the surface.

It's like finding someone who will love you no matter what—being found by them.

A treasure is something worth living for as well as dying for. That's why it's called a treasure. That's why nothing else matters. That's why everyone is still looking for it.

If we are going to find the treasure, we are going to need some clues. This world is a big acre and "somewhere" could be anywhere.

3

Evangelical Dilemma

It's Hard to Believe What You Don't Believe

"Go therefore and make disciples of all the nations."
(Matthew 28:19)

Marching orders. The Commander has spoken and we loyal followers fall in line. Left... Left... Left, Right, Left. Whatever else they might mean, these orders don't imply inaction. "Go" is a simple concept and not easily confused. It doesn't mean wait or stop, it means "Charge!"

So us faithful followers with a cause greater than ourselves, bolstered on by the promise of a better life beyond the grave, march on. "Onward Christian Soldiers, marching as to war..." says it all.

"Marching on, marching for Christ count everything as loss..." goes the old hymn. In the face of enormous adversity, Christians are called to soldier on. "Thy kingdom come. Thy will be done" (Matthew 6:10) said Jesus Himself. Two thousand years of A.D. history has already made the case. Expect insurmountable odds. You'll feel as though you're in a war, not a game.

There will be casualties. Attrition is inevitable. Collateral damage. Friendly fire accidents. Even "crucified with Christ" (Galatians 2:20), according to the apostle Paul.

There is a job to be done and Christians have been called to do it: "make disciples of all the nations" (Matthew 28:19). That's the mission in the Great Commission. People who aren't disciples are intended to become disciples. They are to stop whatever else they are doing and begin doing what disciples do.

That means they must know what disciples do and why, which means somebody has to tell them. This means they will be asked to listen to something new which, though they don't realize it, is actually good news.

So Christians go and tell the Good News. They always have; they always will. But here's the rub: to most people the Good News doesn't sound very good.

Christians are stuck with a mission and with an indifferent response. To be a Christian you have to believe. If you are not a Christian you are being asked to believe what you don't believe, or haven't heard, or don't understand. So libraries are full of books written about why believing the Good News is good news — is such good news.

We mistakenly think that if the moment is just right and the room dark enough with the person facing in the right direction, when the door is opened a crack, even for a few seconds, then the light on the other side might stream through so brightly that the unbeliever might walk over to the door, push it open further, and just walk into another room and finally see the light. They'll see that the Gospel really is good news. Frequently they don't. It's still good news, but they just don't see it.

Telling the Good News is the job and it certainly is a big job. Think about how much work it must be to run a newspaper. Getting any news right is tricky and presenting it well is a difficult profession. "All the news that's fit to print" isn't always fit to print and even if it were, many people only read the sports section, the comics, business pages, or advertisements.

But the Good News is supposed to be good for everyone and, unless you don't get out much, you already know that "everyone" isn't interested.

And so, Christians—at least those who intend to fulfill the Great Commission—have a mission to convey the truth about the Gospel to people with other things they would rather do than listen. We Christians keep trying to find people who are willing to be convinced that what we believe is true while their beliefs are not.

If some of those people were *willing* to change their minds before they *actually* changed their minds, then the job of convincing them that the Good News is good wouldn't be so bad. The percentages might go up.

A concrete example may be useful. Let's say Little Billy insists on pouring his own drink at the dinner table. Mom and Dad know that the lid will fall off and the contents will spill if the pitcher is tipped too steeply, but Little Billy is clueless. Clueless means not knowing that you don't know. So Little Billy dumps the whole pitcher on the table. After they clean up the mess, Little Billy still needs a drink. Instead of "I'll do it." Little Billy now says, "I'll help." Probably because he recognizes that there is more to it than he has yet to comprehend.

Jesus said, "Unless you... become like children, you

shall not enter the kingdom of heaven" (Matthew 18:3). We easily overlook the fact that Little Billy only asked for help after he realized he could not do it himself. Perhaps getting an invitation from Little Billy to present the Good News is a prerequisite for conveying it effectively.

Yet we keep on trying to find people who are willing to be convinced that what they believe may not be true. We've identified several potential methods to achieve this. One is to tell everyone as efficiently as possible such as in a production-oriented, mass-market approach. Or we may try a segmented, targeted appeal. We would use the sports section, the comics, the business pages and the advertise-ments. Eventually, everyone would get a chance to hear the news and the obligation is fulfilled. Or maybe spam could become the next great evangelical tool. We would never miss an opportunity to deliver the message. We make a good attempt to close every sale. We appeal to any and all by every means available so that some may be saved.

Before exploring all of these possibilities, it might be appropriate to officially recognize that the system could use some tweaking. The potential for improvement is a forgone conclusion. Whether it's because culture is constantly changing and Christianity must adapt or because Christianity is being changed along with culture and must retrench, most participants would agree that evangelical efforts are in need of refinement.

Otherwise, they wouldn't always be refining them.

Maybe tweaking isn't a good choice of words. Maybe

renovation is better. Maybe something really has gone awry, leaked in, and tainted the water. Like polluting the Water of Life, so to speak. Like they did in Corinth and Galatia or other places where good words were misused. Pollution happens occasionally and when it does, it's subtle and it doesn't seem so bad.

It's only noticed after it begins to produce some pretty pathetic results. Eventually it becomes so bad in so many places that somebody finally climbs up on top of a house and yells, "Hey, wait a minute!"

So, hey, wait a minute!

4

Unwelcome Witness

So Much to Say, so Few Who Listen

"I send you out as sheep in the midst of wolves… "
(Matthew 10:16)

"Not good." Confirmed my suspicions.

Seven young men and I sat quietly around the cabin, the dim light competing with shadows to illuminate a glance or a flicker of interest. My question hung in the silence, and then bored into their thoughts, stirring unpleasant memories and emotions. They didn't move at first. Preoccupation had overwhelmed all their self-consciousness. My question wasn't hard but it did require a thoughtful answer. There were many ways for them to say the answer. They tried to find one that was better than the rest.

Here's what I had asked them: "What kind of response do you get when you try to share the Good News of Jesus Christ with your friends at school?"

The expression of the boy who answered read *terrible*. So did the catch in his voice, his lowered eyes, and the slow shaking of his head. *Awful. Hopeless. Useless*. Other words were barely concealed beneath the surface of "Not good."

The other boys nodded their heads in agreement. They may have only glimpsed the truth but they recognized it well. It was enough.

"Not good." No dissenting voice. The motion carried.

Everyone in the room seemed to wish that there were

some other answer. Yet there it was. The boys seemed relieved to have it on the table, but they weren't sure what to do with it now that it was.

"It's not easy to be a Christian and stand up for what you believe." One boy broke the silence. "Christians are made fun of a lot."

"I don't always know the right answers and I feel so embarrassed," confessed another. "Maybe we need a class on how to prove that Jesus is God's Son."

Now they began to open up.

"Most people just think we're kind of weird."

"It's not a very good way to make friends and be popular."

Others they talked to were often disinterested, irritated, and sometimes even contemptuous of their efforts to fulfill the Great Commission. (I could see that, surrounded by friends who share your beliefs, rejection could be tolerated pretty well.)

There were still occasional successes, but not many. Occasional success is like golf. But they were like avid golfers who forever practice in pursuit of a perfect golf shot. Being on the outside was the price they were willing to pay for the privilege of knowing the truth and wanting to spread it. Few evangelistic efforts ever produce a hole in one.

These young men were convinced that to be a Christian they had to accept searing ridicule and subtle rejection. They must be willing to face the scorn of the world as they boldly proclaimed the message of Life and God's Kingdom.

But no one wants to be rejected. That is particularly true of teenagers.

"You can't love God and love the world too," one of them declared with a note of confidence that sounded a little too much like resignation.

The mission, for some of these guys, had become a quest to learn all the facts and arguments in support of Christianity. When the moment came, they hoped not to "look like an idiot," as one put it.

Clearly, these boys thought it was important to avoid as many sinful habits as possible. If the message was going to be credible, the life of the messenger must meet a higher standard. Not to mention that some things are "just bad for you, or illegal, or whatever."

Misery sure loves company and as this rag tag batch of believers warmed up to the topic, they began a list of things they were sure most Christians don't do. Underage drinking or hanging out with underage drinkers, especially those who drive, was a no-brainer. So was premarital sex although the line wasn't exactly clear as to where it should be drawn. Internet porn, explicit movies, raunchy lyrics, foul language around other Christians, stealing (except maybe MP3 files) and on and on.

The point was, of course, that to be identified as a Christian, one had to fit, or at least aspire to fit, into a certain mold. The mold was, in part, being willing to defend such uptight behavior on the grounds of "good morals" which Christians should have and may think non-Christians lack.

The more I thought about it, the more I realized that I had learned some important facts during that time in the cabin with those young men.

I learned that they considered themselves morally better than they considered their non-Christian friends, but they still resented being ostracized and ignored.

They wanted to be able to answer any questions and win any arguments about God, but they were frustrated by frequent failure.

They wanted to effectively convey the truth of the Gospel as they knew it, but they were intimidated by consistently poor results.

They agreed that all of the above was what it means to follow Jesus Christ in the world today, and they gravitated towards others just like themselves for friendship and acceptance.

The ones who hadn't given up, that is.

Were their parents having a similar experience? Did being older and wiser change everything? How does the message of the Gospel fly at work and in the neighborhood? How do most adults deal with indifference or hostility?

I wondered only long enough to remember for myself.

I remembered classes on how to share my faith. It used to be called "Lifestyle Evangelism" or "Warm Market Witnessing." Nowadays it is referred to as having an "Authentic Christian Witness." Euphemisms abound.

Whether it's The Four Spiritual Laws, the Jesus Film, a Christmas program, Easter service, a convenient wedding, or a funeral with a captive audience, working the miraculous message into the words of the program has become job number one for believers. Frequently, the world at large turns a deaf ear. Or they hear and brush it off.

Face it, the odds of a successful conversion as a result of any given conversation is probably worse than selling vitamins for a multilevel marketing company. The percentages just aren't there. The perceptions of the target audience really aren't much different either. A bold in-your-face presentation of the Good News is usually met with embarrassment. So the march goes on to repackage the message and fine tune the technique.

The percentages still aren't there.

Christians must conclude, if they are honest with themselves, that the message of eternal life and peace with God is mostly uninteresting and obnoxious to the average person. The One Hope of the One Way to be saved by the Only Son of God is frequently a bother and an interruption, if it's noticed at all.

So, the neighbor doesn't want to hear it. The boss doesn't want to hear it. The employee may listen politely but doesn't care either. Neither does the stranger in the park, the relative across town, or the bum under the overpass. Not the coach. Not the teacher. Not the dentist, the butcher, the baker, or the candlestick maker. The Good News is bad news, or worse, no news. Besides, who cares? Maybe that's the big question.

Who really cares?

5

False God

Worship at the Altar of Empty Words

"Always learning and never able to come to the knowledge of the truth." (2 Timothy 3:7)

As our supersonic T-38 Talon approaches for landing, the twenty-two-year-old Air Force Academy graduate at the controls sweats profusely. It's over one hundred degrees Fahrenheit in the desert as he hurtles the 12,000-pound machine toward what looks at the moment to be an insignificant piece of concrete. His goal is to get the tires on the pavement with enough still in front of him to stop the high performance jet. This is complicated by the fact that the airplane is still heavy with fuel, he's unable to use any flaps to reduce the approach speed, and he has never attempted this before.

I'm the instructor in the back seat and have been here dozens of times. I know exactly where the student pilot will forget to raise the nose of the jet to break the sink rate. I know just when the student will forget to add thrust to hold airspeed. I know that even if the student does remember all that, he still probably won't pull the power back in time to touch down in the first half of the runway. I know exactly how fast five seconds can go by at 200 knots and 20 feet above the ground.

I also know how far I can let this sweating young man go before I have to say "I've got it." and then light both of the afterburners (for attention-getting emphasis) and save both our lives once more so the kid can try it again.

Now the student studied hard. He knows all the speeds and parameters. He did his homework so the preflight briefing went very well. This young lieutenant is a highly motivated officer who dreams of fighter jets and aerial combat. He can't wait to be at "the tip of the spear." It's just that there is more to learning this stuff than information.

Some people say that the goal of flight school is to fill up your bag of experience before your bag of luck is empty. They say you don't really know until you know.

That's why people in Missouri say, "show me." That's why in first grade Show-and-Tell was always more fun than just Tell could ever be. That's why a picture is worth a thousand words and in flight school a good "demo" is worth a thousand debriefs. So, where did some Christians get the silly idea that merely thinking and talking about God, Jesus, and Love was sufficient?

One translation of the Bible says Adam knew Eve before their children were born. There is the hint of more than just information in that particular "knowing," as anyone with a similar experience will already know. Guess what? Knowing truth that sets you free involves experience too.

The idea that truth can be known entirely by proposition is insupportable. Truth about anything is much more substantial than that and human experience much more complex. Words and ideas about anything are only useful to the degree that they accurately convey truth about it. Truth itself, in all of its abundance, beauty, complexity, depth, and enormity is not contained within words. Words about truth are important but not sufficient. Truth alone is sufficient.

My Dad used to say to me, "Talk's cheap, Son." Then he and I would go to work on some job that needed to be done and then I would understand.

So here we are, products of a culture in which information has been elevated to unbelievable heights. This amazing modern era has been built upon the accumulation and proliferation of information. In this information age, we have grown so accustomed to a pathological preoccupation with information that we barely notice what we've lost.

But what if there is more to knowledge than information?

Then, what if we confuse mere information with understanding?

And what if belief depends on understanding?

Nearly everyone knows what it sounds like to say or hear the words "I love you." The definitions of those three words are unambiguous. But how well do you understand what it means to be really loved? Not until your dad gives you his kidney, your wife forgives your obstinacy for the 5000th time, or a friend stays with you in the hospital until you're well do you begin to understand how much those words can mean. "Greater love has no one than this, that he lay down his life for a friend." (John 15:13) True, of course.

Words and information are fantastic. We couldn't live without them because they communicate life. Only when words and information are mistaken for the things that they represent does it begin to unravel. Talking about being on time is rarely an adequate substitute for punctuality. Practice is in actuality what makes perfect. The couch potatoes who know so much about sports or politics or this old house may be in for a big surprise when they finally get off the couch. Words are about life, but they are not life itself.

Sometimes we are unaware of how mistaken we are. We often know so little about so much and yet we think we know so much. We blithely talk about things we don't understand very well. We claim to have all the answers to the questions honest people ask about deep things while we only scratch the surface. We get all the facts right and some-how miss the point, which was that the facts were about something real, and good, and true.

Jesus said, "You search the Scriptures, because you think that in them you have eternal life; and it is those that bear witness of Me; and you are unwilling to come to Me, that you may have life" (John 5:13). Empty words. Noisy gongs. Clanging symbols. Houses built on sand.

Christian information has been on the rise since Gutenberg invented the printing press and isn't going to stop any time soon. The words are important. Proposition is crit-ical. True words about truth are needed now as much as ever. But Christians can be meticulous about getting the facts right without even applying them. So here's the prob-lem: when words or information become idolized to the point of neglecting the "weightier provisions" (Matthew 23:23) we worship at the altar of a false god.

The need for truth in all of its fullness and glory cannot be neglected without consequence. The god of empty words, no matter how true and correct the words, cannot deliver on his promises. This god cannot adequately convey truth, convict hearts, transform lives, or instill and sustain the life of the Spirit.

When the charge of hypocrisy is leveled at the Church, some embrace it too willingly. They already know we are sinners "saved by grace" (Ephesians 2:8). They are secure in the possession of true words and, apparently, impervious. Within her ranks, though, are many who realize something is wrong.

The best argument *for* the truth of Christianity is always a Christian. Unfortunately, so is the best argument *against* the truth of Christianity. When enough people have become smugly complacent, when they have all the right answers but don't bother to live them, when the only face they show the world is judgmental, self-righteous, intolerant, and arrogant, the verdict is in.

"The one who does not love does not know God, for God is love."

(1 John 4:8)

"For the one who does not love his brother whom he has seen, cannot love God whom he has not seen."

(1 John 4:20)

"He who has the Son has the life, He who does not have the Son of God does not have the life."

(1 John 5:12)

Tragically, a false god equals no life.

So then, which prevails if correct doctrine and love are in contest? Love or doctrine? Or are they ever really in contest?

Isn't it preferable to be wronged rather than not love? And isn't that correct doctrine?

If someone could sum up "the Law and the Prophets" in just a few words, would love be among those words?

When everything else fails, won't love remain?

Not many are willing to look this carefully in the mirror. Some may look and see, but quickly walk away and forget. A few will stare intently, and when they do, perhaps they will begin to clearly see the purpose and the goal.

The apostle Paul writes to Timothy: "The goal of our instruction is love from a pure heart and a good conscience and a sincere faith" (1 Timothy 1:5). That means love can never be relegated to the leftover department. It can't be what we do only after we expend every available resource to nail down the facts.

The crazy thing is that everyone already knows this. The false god is easily unmasked at every turn. This nonsense is only embraced by well meaning Christians who live in total denial. Trying so hard to say it well, yet resigned to never live it well, they deny its power. (2 Timothy 3:5). Do they really believe that they could understand it from hearing only? Do they really think others will somehow understand it from hearing only?

"And everyone who hears these words of Mine, and does not act upon them, will be like a foolish man, who built his house upon the sand" (Matthew 7:26). A foolish altar to a false god.

"The Word became flesh, and dwelt among us, and we beheld His glory, glory as of the only begotten of the Father, full of grace and truth" (John 1:14). The true God became flesh, *so* we would understand.

"...speaking the truth in love" (Ephesians 4:15) is not a choice we get to make. It's not an option for us to choose. It's a statement of fact.

There is no other way to convey Truth.

6

Upside Down

New Perspective for a Topsy-Turvy World

"Blessed are those who have been persecuted for the sake of righteousness, for theirs is the kingdom of heaven." (Matthew 5:10)

S ome of the boys in the cabin sincerely thought they had been persecuted. They had been left out, picked on, picked last, overlooked, mocked, rejected, and hurt. But I did need to ask a few questions to help clarify the situation.

"Hey, this sounds pretty bad. Help me get this straight. You say you're being singled out because you are a Christian?

"That's right."

"You're suffering at the hands of your peers because you want to follow Jesus Christ?"

"Yes."

"I know it happens, but could you give me some more detail here? Do you mean to tell me that, because you are living a life of obedience to the Son of God, you've been persecuted?"

"That's right."

"So tell me, which of the commands of Jesus are causing such problems for you? Is it because someone struck you and you turned the other cheek?"

"No."

"Then was it that you were asked for your coat and you gave somebody your shirt as well?"

"No."

"Did someone need to borrow some money and you just gave it to them instead?"

"What? What are you talking about?"

"Were you robbed and just let the thief keep the stuff after you caught him?"

"Are you kidding me?"

"Well, what was it then? You said that following Jesus had put you in a tough spot and I'm trying to figure out if I can be of any help. What did you do that caused them to reject you?"

"I was sharing the gospel."

"Well, that's great. The Bible says very clearly that we should always be ready to give an answer for the hope that we have. What kind of questions were you answering?"

"There were no questions. They didn't even want to hear about it."

"Oh, I see."

"They don't listen when I try to tell them or they make fun of what I say."

"Really? Are these friends of yours always so rude?"

"They're not my friends. And yes, they're very rude, especially when I try to talk about God."

"So the times that you're being persecuted are usually when you get in these unwelcome discussions?"

"Pretty much."

" OK. When you're not talking about God to these people, are you showing them what it means to follow Jesus?"

"What do you mean?'

Before I knew what had happened, I had launched myself into an impassioned rant.

"I mean do you find the stinky loser in your class that nobody likes and become his one very best friend? Do you pay attention to the needs of others and always consider them as more important than your own needs?"

"Do you keep your word and forgive others when they don't? Do you prefer to be the one who gets left out, rather than allowing someone else endure it? Can you even remember the last time you returned good for evil or a blessing for a curse? Do you accept criticism well and take great care to not be judgmental?"

"Do you stay awake late at night trying to figure out how to make someone who hates you feel better about themselves? Do you forgive?"

"Please, help me understand what it is about following Jesus Christ that the rest of the world finds so repulsive."

"I don't know what you're talking about," came the defensive dodge.

"What I mean is, maybe you are being singled out for ridicule, but it might not be because you're following and obeying Jesus. It might be something else about you."

"Like what?"

"Perhaps you were being inconsiderate. Maybe you need to learn some basic social skills. They might just find you arrogant and self-centered. Insincerity is very hard to hide. If you really don't care about a person they might pick up on that. Nobody wants to hang out with an obnoxious selfish jerk."

"Hey, that seems a little harsh."

I softened a bit, "I was just exploring some possibilities. You might actually love those people but just not be very good at showing it. Why don't you try to convince them that you really do care about them first and then see what happens next?"

Equivocation came next, "But I show them that I care about them by telling them about Jesus."

"Is that all Jesus said to do? Did He just say preach the gospel?"

"No, He said make disciples too."

"Anything else? "

"Well, He said teach them to obey His commands."

"That's right. So lets go back for a minute. What sort of things did he command?"

"Well, there were lots of them."

"Sure. Things like turn the other cheek and walk the extra mile and give away your shirt too if they ask for your coat. Things like loan without expecting to be repaid and give whenever you are asked and let thieves keep what they steal. Pray for your enemies. Always return good for evil. Return a blessing for a curse. He commanded us to lay up treasures in heaven. He said, Deny yourself, take up your cross, and follow Me. What kind of person would live that kind of life?"

Nobody blinked.

"So, you're saying that's how I'm supposed to make disciples? That's asking a lot. I would have to change nearly everything about the way I live to even begin to do those kinds of things. I'm not even sure that I could do it. Isn't all that just something to think about and maybe a goal to try for?"

"No. Those are His commands. Not His goals, His commands. He did say, however, that you should count the cost before you decide. No sense starting, if you know up front that you really have no intention of finishing. It sounds to me like you might be counting."

"I am counting, but this is extreme and a little bit unbelievable. Besides, I'm not sure what all this would accomplish. Why haven't I ever heard this before?"

"You have heard it before. And to begin with, it might convince some people that you really do care about them. It would make them wonder why any person would live such a crazy unselfish life. You might have to answer a few questions that come up about the kind of hope that you have. They might even want to listen to you for a change."

The guys in the cabin were listening now.

"Imagine for a moment that Jesus knows exactly what He is talking about and exactly how to accomplish His goals. Pretend with me for a minute, if you're not quite sure yet, that the Great Commission is really a brilliantly conceived yet simple strategy that will accomplish everything He wants to accomplish. And imagine, if you can, that it's also more complicated and comprehensive than you'll ever know."

"Jesus may expect His followers to actually do what He told them. He may intend to use those things to build the kingdom of heaven."

Light bulbs began to come on one by one. You could see a faint glimmer of recognition stirring inside.

"Here's the scenario: You wake up every morning and know exactly what God wants you to do with your life, wherever you are. Love Him and love your neighbor. Anyone could be your neighbor. And when you do that, you are carrying out His plan. Involvement in the kingdom of heaven is part of every day of your life. It's right here, waiting for you to participate. Every time you obey Him, God would use you to accomplish His plans and His purpose in His kingdom."

"By loving all the people you encounter, you become like God in a way; His very own children who are becoming like Him. He is kind, patient, and forgiving, and truthful, fair, and merciful. You could become like that. Jesus knew that would happen. He might find it useful. It might even have been the plan all along. Actions might speak louder than empty words."

By now, looks of vacant stupidity had been replaced with expressions of hopeful comprehension.

"How many times would you have to trust God and live such an upside down life before it became routine?"

"How many times would you struggle to overcome selfishness and self-interest before you could do it without thinking?"

"How many times would you have to see God clearly at

work through these choices before you realized that you were part of something bigger than you ever dreamed?"

"Not very many times, I think." blurted one of the boys without thinking.

"Did anyone ever tell you that God intends for you to play a critical role in the lives of the people around you?"

"Did anyone ever mention that the big plan is for people to see God's character and love through His children?"

"Did you ever hear that the kingdom of heaven is right here at your fingertips? Did you know that when you obey Jesus and love like He loves, God works through you right here, right now?"

"Did anyone ever happen to make it really clear to you that this is His plan?"

"No one ever said it exactly like that before," volunteered one of the boys.

"Well that's the whole enchilada. All the other complicated stuff is a part of it. This is what you *obey* when you *go into all the world*. Without this, the rest is just noise."

"Listen guys. Someday there will be no more tears, no more sadness, no more death, no more loneliness, no more hatred, and no more evil. But for now, God's plan is that His very own children reflect His love right here, right now, right in the face of all this evil. Children like you, who are becoming more like Him.

7

Living Sacrifice

Mortality Putting on Immortality

"For by one offering He has perfected for all time those who are sanctified." (Hebrews 10:14)

There is an amazing life of *impossible love* that is available to any human being who will abandon everything else in order to possess it. If you have ever been loved or been in love, you have touched it. If you have ever given yourself entirely to another person for their benefit and your loss, you have tasted it. If you have ever witnessed this kind of selfless life in action, you may have been captivated by wonder or helpless adoration.

This heroic experience is the pinnacle of human existence. It's the pinnacle because its price is a life given away for another person. This gift is a present possibility in every moment of every day, but it can never be coerced.

Entry into this way of life appears to be a paradox. From the perspective of selfish survival and personal achievement, the idea is insanity. It is incompatible with selfish ego. It cannot coexist with pride or greed.

This life involves gaining by giving, winning by losing, it's backwards, ridiculous, and upside-down.

This life is counterintuitive, countercultural, and seems counterproductive.

It's the antithesis of survival of the fittest because it's living by dying.

It's a path to freedom that requires us to choose slavery.

We all recognize this kind of life when we see it. We are exhilarated when we experience it. This elusive life of love, passion, and purpose we all crave appears just beyond our grasp. Though we desire it, we fear it because to achieve such a life will ultimately cost us our own.

Life without this kind of love is only a selfish subhuman existence. Though it occasionally sparkles like a precious gem, it usually results in an endless search for a treasure—a treasure we know is there, but never seem to find.

Sometimes this battle for a life of love seems like a struggle between me and myself. It's confusing and even gets a little comical. This war inside of me, how will I know who is winning? If it's me against myself, might there be a clinical term to describe my condition?

When I finally prevail (which, of course, I will), how can I be sure which of me has won? Or maybe I can never really win because I have to lose to win. So then, is that a tie? Do I have some kind of evil twin or just a bothersome psychological disorder? Would some kind of professional help be warranted?

I find I am not likely to address this conundrum seriously or effectively unless I can clearly identify all the players involved. To say all of them are "me" doesn't seem to help.

We perceive this as a paradox because we don't usually think of ourselves as competing entities. We don't see two bodies; we see one. We don't hear two voices; we hear only one. One personality. One brain. One life. But we do argue with ourselves over choices. We do choose, and then second-guess our own choice. We sometimes even regret what we have chosen. Perhaps, we just can't decide at all. One thing is for sure. We have competing loyalties, preferences, and appetites all wrapped up inside of a single person.

In my case, it feels like part of me wants to do one thing and another part of me doesn't. I disappoint myself. I surprise myself. I amaze myself. After further examination, I find this situation to be quite revealing.

When we examine the evidence before us, we discover that there are at least two parts to each of us. There is a conversation going on inside our heads (or our hearts) that we must listen to, and between which we must choose.

First, there is the part of me that is not much different than a very smart animal. Let's call him "Brilliant Ape." He is a creature of *physical* desires and appetites. He is controlled and influenced by emotions, hungers, cravings, instinct, and habits. Body chemistry and brain chemistry determine his behavior. Because of Brilliant Ape's complex brain, his desires, and needs can become rather convoluted and sophisticated. The fact remains that he just wants what he wants when he wants it, and he's always trying to get it. Egocentric. To him, life is all about Brilliant Ape.

Second, there is the part of me that reflects the image of God. This part is spiritual even though it may result from physiology. This part of me has often been referred to as "Ghost in the Machine." It is controlled and influenced by *nonphysical* entities. Personality forces such as ideas, values, meaning, and morality have weight. *Should* and *ought* influence behavior. The primary motivation is love, justice, mercy, rights, morality, or some other higher order, nonphysical thing. To Ghost in the Machine, life consists of more than self.

But notice how each person has an identity that is separate from these and chooses between them. There is a part of us all that decides, and those decisions then determine our life.

The Bible suggests that Ghost in the Machine is dormant or dead. We are now aware of the sad fact that Brilliant Ape is running the show. The Bible says Adam and Eve blew it for all of us. As their descendants, we get little or no help from "Ghost in the Machine."

We are left with Brilliant Ape in charge, always demanding his way and his satisfaction. As a result, we are crippled, selfish, and try to make sense out of a world packed with meaning and purpose but without Ghost in the Machine to help figure it out. Like a child who wants to know why he can't have chocolate cake for breakfast every morning, we're without a higher perspective. A faulty conclusion is inevitable. To a man with only a hammer, everything looks like a nail.

Then along comes Jesus Christ—a human being controlled entirely by Ghost in the Machine. In Him, we see Brilliant Ape as an obedient servant to the image of God within. In Jesus Christ, we see God clearly as a man. We also see how badly we may have fallen short of our destiny. We can glimpse what we were meant to be like.

We recognize the treasure and we can't help but wonder.

Is Brilliant Ape all there is? Could Ghost in the Machine live again? Can humankind ever again reflect the image of God?

Christianity is all about God who wakes up Ghost in the Machine and helps me subdue Brilliant Ape. Selfish, egotistical, subhuman Brilliant Ape must now become a willing slave to Ghost in the Machine who is loving, righteous, holy and bears the image of God.

Christianity is made up of people who have been brought back to life as it was meant to be. (This may not include everyone who merely claims to be a Christian.) It's people who are in the process of becoming more and more like Jesus Christ—who is just like God. They are people who have experienced the Ghost in the Machine at work again in their lives and think it's good news. This good news sounds like bad news to Brilliant Ape.

That's the story of Christianity: Ghost in the Machine can live again... forever.

That's the story of the Treasure.

That's why loving God and loving other people is so important.

Any Brilliant Ape can read the Bible and get all the facts right.

Only Ghost in the Machine can live it.

The following words written by the apostle Paul from

Corinth are worth reading carefully again with these characters in mind. To get a clear picture of what Paul says, replace "flesh" with Brilliant Ape and replace "Spirit" with Ghost in the machine.

Paul writes about this struggle within and what it reveals about us in a letter to the church in Rome:

> "For what the Law could not do, weak as it was through the flesh, God did: sending His own Son in the likeness of sinful flesh and as an offering for sin, He condemned sin in the flesh, in order that the requirement of the Law might be fulfilled in us, who do not walk according to the flesh, but according to the Spirit.
>
> For those who are according to the flesh set their minds on the things of the flesh, but those who are according to the Spirit, the things of the Spirit.
>
> For the mind set on the flesh is death, but the mind set on the Spirit is life and peace, because the mind set on the flesh is hostile toward God; for it does not subject itself to the law of God, for it is not even able to do so; and those who are in the flesh cannot please God.
>
> However, you are not in the flesh but in the Spirit, if indeed the Spirit of God dwells in you. But if anyone does not have the Spirit of Christ, he does not belong to Him.
>
> And if Christ is in you, though the body is dead

because of sin, yet the spirit is alive because of righteousness.

But if the Spirit of Him who raised Jesus from the dead dwells in you, He who raised Christ Jesus from the dead will also give life to your mortal bodies through His Spirit who indwells you.

So then, brethren, we are under obligation, not to the flesh, to live according to the flesh — for if you are living according to the flesh, you must die; but if by the Spirit you are putting to death the deeds of the body, you will live.

For all who are being led by the Spirit of God, these are sons of God."

(Romans 8:3-14)

So how can we begin to live *by* the Spirit? What must we do differently each day to begin experiencing this new spiritual life for ourselves? How do we begin this transformation?

The answer is closer than we imagine. It's right here at our fingertips.

We can set our hope entirely on something beyond ourselves and yet somehow familiar. We can look to our own nature and the world around us for clues about the treasure we've lost. We can experience and share the unexpected familiar fantasy of goodness unwarranted and unearned.

We can begin to live a kind of life so upside down, counterintuitive, and driven by love that we begin to resemble creatures from another world. We can boldly embrace the guiding principle of the entire universe and beyond.

We can become the very children of "The God Who Loves."

8

Fruit Phenomenon

Good Fruit from a Good Tree

"But the fruit of the Spirit is love, joy, peace, patience, kindness, goodness, faithfulness, gentleness, self control; against such things there is no law." (Galatians 5:22-23)

"I hate Christians."

It was more of an evasive maneuver than an outright attack. It could have been intended to end the conversation before it began. Somehow, the Boeing 757 Captain had guessed that I, his First Officer for the next four days, was willing to talk about spiritual matters. The Captain, hoped to set the tone before any further discussion ensued.

"Why is that?" came my sincere question from the right seat. "Is there some particular reason you feel that way?"

"Yeah. Christians are emotionally crippled and intellectually compromised. They have a need to explain everything in terms of the Bible. They rely on faith and dogma instead of using reason to follow the evidence. I can't stand people who won't follow the evidence wherever it leads. I think like a scientist and I'm committed to rational thought. Christians refuse to be rational."

This is going to be fun, I thought. Then I asked, "You've given this a lot of thought, haven't you?"

"Yes I have."

"Isn't there anything you admire about Christians?"

"No."

"Oh, come on. What about their willingness to take abuse from guys like you for what they believe?" I asked with a smile intended to convey some levity and reduce the tension. "Isn't that something to admire? I mean someone who has the integrity to hold onto their convictions in the face of such harsh criticism must at least have some character."

"Not if they ignore their minds to hold onto their convictions. There is nothing to admire in that."

"Good point. But what if they are convinced, somehow, that it's all true? What if they examined all the evidence and concluded that Jesus Christ really is the Son of the Living God and that He rose from the dead. If they've done that, you can certainly criticize their conclusions but you must also see the character it takes to stand firm with such an unpopular view."

"Well, maybe."

"Oh, give us a break. We're stuck. It's what we believe. If I caved in to pressure from you or anybody else, then that would be contemptible and completely dishonest. Even you wouldn't respect that. You don't have to agree to recognize or admire honesty."

"OK, they're honest, but they're also ignorant. They can't let go of blind faith long enough to find truth. Rather than figure things out, they just say, "God did it." That's what I mean by intellectual compromise."

"So you think guys like the Apostle Paul who wrote half of the New Testament, Thomas Aquinas, G. K. Chesterson, C.

S. Lewis, Sir Isaac Newton, and Jesus Christ himself were all intellectually compromised? That's a bit of a stretch, isn't it?"

"Well listen, I'm stuck too. I can't just ignore rational thought and blame everything on God. There has to be a physical explanation. To just say 'I don't know so uh... God!' is not an option for me. Science and rational thought demand an answer and then follow the facts until they find the answer. That's the only way I can approach life, so I guess I'm the one who's stuck here. I'm stuck with the fact that cause and effect rule the physical world and I can't pretend otherwise. As far as I can tell, cause and effect are the only keys that will ever unlock the mysteries of the universe."

The Captain was right, of course. Captains are always right—that's how they get to be Captains. This one just didn't know how right he was.

We may not understand all the physical wonders of our universe, but we do understand the world is a cause and effect operation. Though exact explanations may elude us at times, this particular fact does not escape our notice.

It doesn't matter whether the scientific quest is pursued through the lens of the most powerful telescope out to the limits of time and space or through the lens of the most sophisticated microscope down to the quantum peculiarities of tiny spaces. Cause and effect are the magic decoder rings for deciphering all of creation. Proposal becomes experiment, which becomes theory, which becomes physical law. Truth is discovered like a buried treasure that was there all along.

We can see clearly that the Creator has placed His own

signature on all of His amazing work. This cause and effect style is the Artist's very own trademark.

> "For since the creation of the world His invisible attributes, His eternal power and divine nature, have been clearly seen, being understood through what has been made, so that they are without excuse."
>
> (Romans 1:20)

So then, nature reflects the very nature of God Himself.

Year after year, for centuries, even longer, apple trees have produced apples. For the foreseeable future, this remarkable coincidence will continue. When a guy walks into an apple orchard and picks an apple from a tree, he can be absolutely sure that he's picking it from an apple tree. That's because apple trees produce apples. Other fruit trees produce other fruit. Nut trees produce nuts. We would have to be nuts to expect any thing else.

If apples always come from apple trees, then apples are a clue. We know chickens come from eggs and eggs come from chickens. We also know that for every action there is an equal and opposite reaction. These effects always come from a cause. Effects are clues to the cause. This is a cause and effect universe and so we have lots of clues.

Now this could get exciting. Maybe we aren't clueless after all. If this works out well, we may end up running around looking for clues like a funny little band of crazed monkeys.

We may even find a treasure.

We know that the pathway leading to the secrets of the physical world is paved with cause and effect. We observe the results to discover the cause. This is orderly, fair, dependable, and precise. It makes sense. It's useful. In a word, it's brilliant.

Doesn't it make sense that such a clever system might be used in other ways too? Couldn't the Creator work His "signature style" into relationships and psychology, into economics and politics? Wouldn't it help explain why cause and effect can be seen so clearly in many other *nonphysical* ways?

We have discovered this consistency built into our personal relationships and dealings with people. We have many ways of saying the same thing: "What goes around comes around," "If you want to play, you've got to pay," "You make your own luck," or "Well, he got what he asked for." We shouldn't be surprised. The same cause and effect rules apply.

To take this observation further, we need a solid place to begin. What must be done first is to establish some facts. The facts could be a list of desirable human traits that have withstood the tests of time and the full range of human experience. They need to be things we can follow to their cause. We could restrict it to what the common experience of all humanity has verified. History would help reveal the consensus. The consensus will be the clue.

Could a comprehensive list of overwhelmingly acceptable attributes be found? If we examine the conclusions of people alive today as well as people who lived in the past, everyone would have a voice in the results. If we could agree on such a list or discover one already assembled, we could begin our search for the source.

In an ancient letter written to friends in a town called Galatia, around AD 49-56, a man wrote the following: "The fruit of the Spirit are love, joy, peace, patience, kindness, goodness, faithfulness, gentleness, self control; against such things there is no law" (Galatians 5:22). This remarkable list may be as close as we ever get to a comprehensive consensus of our potential.

These are the kinds of results we need to examine.

So, if we find the kind of results in life that we treasure, we can try to follow them to their source. We would expect the fruit that we treasure to come from the branches of the tree that *is* the treasure. When we discover the kind of life worth living or discover someone who is living it, we're staring into the face of a big fat clue. It's unavoidable because fruit doesn't just happen. It's caused.

If there are no good clues where you have already looked, why not look somewhere else? It doesn't make sense to look for a cause where there are no effects. If there is no fruit, there is no tree. "If the fruit is bad, then so is the tree" (Matthew 7:17-20). But remember, if the fruit is good then we are on our way to finding the source.

One thing we know for sure about this fruit phenomenon: there's fruit everywhere.

Since this is a cause and effect world, it might be worthwhile to discover what causes good fruit.

9

Super Powers

An Ability Not Normally Associated with Humanity

"The one who does not love does not know God; for God is love." (1 John 4:8)

The dark green '97 Chevy Suburban careened around the icy corner. The steep winding road twisted and dodged as though it were a wild animal trying to escape the 7,300-pound beast. The studded tires clawed the slick surface and gripped the edge of the lane on the downhill side of the mountain.

Inside the Suburban, music blared and testosterone surged through the veins of seven teenagers determined to conquer the slopes. Visions of "massive corked sevens" and "rodeo five's" taunted them in their dreams. They planned the attack and hoped to score some "really big air" in the newly groomed half pipe.

Thirty years ago, I too had been a teenager possessed by superhuman aspirations. From the way I was driving, you might think I hadn't changed much. The explanation is that exhilaration had us all by the throat. It felt good to be alive.

We weren't the only ones to ever feel this way. Many before us have had a fantasy about exceeding human limitations in speed, strength, flight, and sight. Some people only fantasize about it. Some actually pursue it. Either way, humankind has dreamed of superior abilities for a very long time.

Movies make the case today. The worldwide box office gross for the Spiderman and Spiderman II movies exceed 1.5 billion dollars. Clearly, someone is thinking about super powers. Flash Gordon, The Incredible Hulk, Spiderman, Superman, Thor, Zeus, Mercury, and Poseidon. A fascination with super heroes goes back for centuries.

I asked the boys if they would answer a question I had entertained ever since I heard it discussed on National Public Radio. "If you could have one super power, which would you pick: the ability to fly or the ability to be invisible? "

"How high can we fly?" was the first question.

"As high as you want," I said, "but remember, the air gets thin up high and you still need to breathe."

"OK, how fast can we go?"

"Until your eyelids peel back so far your eyeballs dry out and you can't see any more."

"What if we fly into a cloud and hit a mountain."

"You're dead. You don't get to be Superman, you just get to fly." I explained.

"Do we have to be invisible all the time?"

"No."

"Good, because you can't really make friends very well if you're invisible."

"When we're invisible, what about our clothes?"

"They are invisible too. So is your watch and shoes."

"Do we make footprints?" came the next query.

"In the snow, yes. On concrete, probably not unless you've been in the mud."

"Can people hear our steps when we walk?"

"Of course, if they can hear your steps now. Look you guys, only one super power. Everything else stays the same. Now pick one and give us your reason."

"Can you imagine the tricks you could land if you could fly? You wouldn't just look like you were defying gravity, you would be."

"I'd pick flying... so I could go anywhere I wanted for free," one boy finally proclaimed.

"If you picked invisibility you wouldn't have to buy a plane ticket so you could be invisible and fly for free too," countered another.

"Flying would be boring after awhile since you only get to do it alone... I'd pick being invisible."

"Me too. Invisible would never be boring. You could go anywhere and nobody would even know that you were there."

"Yeah, you could spy on people, and hear and see everything they do and never get caught."

A hush fell over the car as that last thought settled in, *see and hear everything they do...* A mile went by in a flurry of dangerous possibilities.

From the back seat came a matter-of-fact decision, "I better choose flying."

"Why?" I asked.

"I know myself pretty well and, if I were invisible, I would do a lot of things I shouldn't do. After a while, my conscience would be so bad, I'd just be miserable. I guess I have to pick flying."

I parked the car near the ski lodge and the conversation was over. "We're here. Everyone out."

"For what the Law could not do, weak as it was through the flesh, God did..."

(Romans 8:3)

Two years later, while waiting in the airport for a boarding announcement, I scanned the CNN web site for news with my cell phone. The top story made me shudder. Terrorists had again murdered an innocent hostage. Here was a man, whose only crime had been to enter a foreign country to help its people. He had been tortured and executed. The heinous event was distributed over the Internet for the world to watch.

The revulsion I felt at the thought of such evil is indescribable. The tragic story hijacked my mind for the entire flight and even into the early hours of a sleepless morning. How could such a horror ever be made right? *Dear God, please make this stop!* Disgust became anger and then became rage as hatred boiled quickly to consciousness.

My thoughts raced wildly on. One thought stopped me cold. It was an honest question and it kept me up for hours. I wasn't prepared for the answer. I knew what my reaction was to this despicable crime against God and all humanity. What was God's reaction?

This was a brutal torture and a senseless murder. An innocent loved one was crushed and afflicted. Such pain, such sorrow, and such horror. I only felt rage and revulsion. If I could exact payment from these animals, I believe I would. An eye for an eye. A tooth for a tooth. A life for a life. Yet, as I fantasized about revenge, I already knew the answer.

A young Jewish rabbi, at the age of thirty-three years, was beaten bloody and crucified publicly for telling everyone he met that the kingdom of God was present and inviting them to love God and love each other from their hearts. He claimed to have come from God to show the way. He claimed to *be* the way. He was tortured and murdered—and God watched.

There is no room here for equivocation. You can't just explain this away so that it's impotent or easy. There can be no misunderstanding of intent or outcome.

Through his split and swollen lips, he whispered from the core of his battered body. His dry tongue gagged as he sucked in enough air to drive his choking vocal chords. In that moment, the cry of his bursting heart—the one thing that mattered to him the most and the very center of who he was and everything he ever taught—was clear.

With his dying breath, he cried, "Father, forgive them. They don't even know what they are doing." (Luke 23:34 para.)

He knew what they were doing. He knew what *He* was doing. One thing, one incredibly unbelievable superhuman thing: "Love your enemies" (Matthew 5:44, Luke 6:27, 35). I thought I knew what He meant. I thought I could do that. I'm not Superman.

Jesus insists that the only life worth living is like the one He lived. To do that we must exercise a counterintuitive, selfless love that is unbelievable, unnatural, and inhuman. He calls every one of us to be super heroes, to exercise superhuman powers of love. That's it.

That's His solution for everything. His answer for everything. His plan for everything. His purpose for everything. According to Him, love is the single overarching guiding principle of the entire universe and beyond.

"The Kingdom of Heaven is at hand." (Matthew 3:2, 4:17, 10:7)

Everything He taught His followers had superhuman, selfless, sacrificial love at its very core. Love for God and love for man. It's as if Jesus were telling us "God's character is love. I'm His Son. Pay attention." Same song, second verse.

Like a one-trick pony whose only trick is the secret treasure trove of life itself. It's an invitation to participate now, every day, in the purpose and plans of God for all of time and eternity. It's an invitation to become exactly who you were meant to be all along, like a precious buried treasure just waiting to be discovered.

Everything else that masquerades as Christianity, but doesn't have love for God and love for mankind at its center, is a fraud, a sham, or a terrible delusion. If what we call "Christianity" becomes something else, it too will pass away while the Bride of Christ continues to prepare for her wedding day.

One day, everything else will pass away and only faith, hope, and love will remain. (1 Corinthians 13:13)

But the greatest of all superpowers is love.

10

Simple Complexity

A Place to Begin That Has No End

"And she gave birth to her first born son; and she wrapped Him in cloths and laid Him in a feeding trough." (Luke 2:7)

Twenty-seven years ago, I eagerly anticipated another Christmas day. The frivolous trappings of the season were everywhere. The spirits of giving and getting were in the air. Familiar songs and sights whirled around the world from every angle and, like the voices of angels, spread good tidings of great joy. Everyone was ready to celebrate.

On the eve of Christmas Eve, bad tidings of great sorrow crushed my heart and sent me reeling. I suppose I've never been the same.

As Christmas approached fifteen years later, a good friend noticed that an uncharacteristic melancholy had come over me again and he asked why the season affected me so. I hadn't even noticed. After some introspection, I realized that I was deeply troubled by the apparent lack of attention to the only thing that really matters about Christmas. It's when "God became a man," or a baby to be more precise.

Understandably, you might wonder, *why is that the only thing that really matters?* Well, I'll tell you.

Sitting around the tree twenty-seven years ago, going through the motion of opening gifts with an incomplete family, while staring at gifts that would never be opened by a missing father, I was thinking of a funeral to come. The utter hopelessness of a Christmas accompanied by murder is impossible to convey. The juxtaposition of evil and death with the spirit of love and the birth of Christ seemed unnatural then. It is unnatural.

Unless Christmas has an answer for exactly this situation, everything about it is only good feelings and hopeful fantasy. Without an answer for this, Christmas is just another pleasant distraction in a relatively short and hopeless life. It's even worse than that. It's a big lie. How can anyone be joyful about Christmas if it makes promises it can never deliver?

Isn't Christmas about a God who became like us to save us from sin and death? True or false? If true, we have much to celebrate. If false, we have nothing. Apart from the baby in the manger, we must face the fact that "every cradle swings above a grave."

As I think about Christmas now, I still think about a cradle and a grave, but the grave I think about is Jesus' empty grave, so I can really celebrate. At Christmas time the only hope ever offered humanity is before our very eyes even though we may not see. It's on our lips, if not yet in our hearts. It's at our fingertips and only to be grasped.

Such an inelegant description of the meaning of Christmas usually produces a predictable response. To reduce the essence of Christmas to such a brief formula appears too simplistic. It wouldn't be difficult to make a case that there is much more to Christmas than this. Such a case would miss the point.

There are many complicated things to figure out in this world. And no matter how complex they become along the way, in the end much of what we know to be true about reality can be summed up very simply. The incarnation is no exception. As an historical event which took place in time and space, it would be surprising if its meaning could not be captured in simple terms. Its implications, however, are immense.

Albert Einstein's Special Theory of Relativity is a similar example.

$E=MC^2$ for instance is a simple looking formula that even a child can recognize. But what does it mean? Well, E is for energy and MC^2 is for mass times the square of the constant speed of light. Another way to say this might be that all the energy in a thing is equal to its mass times a whopping gigantic number. Everything is made entirely of energy. A lot of energy. See how easy that was? Or how about this explanation? All matter is frozen energy. Simple. $E=MC^2$ just helps us figure out how much energy.

This means that tiny atoms contain huge amounts of energy. So much energy that relatively few atoms could be used to make a very big bomb, power an aircraft carrier, or even provide power for an entire city.

It's a simple equation that anyone can comprehend and yet one that generations of physicists have spent their entire lives applying to the real world.

Until Albert Einstein figured out this simple equation, nobody knew it was so simple. There were many experiments hinting that this might be the case, but no one was able to pull it all together and state it so clearly. When he did that, everything changed.

Simple explanations are often found on the far side of great effort and a lifetime of experience. My wife's ninety-two year old grandfather once offered this succinct advice to a young college student with the temerity to trouble him for words of wisdom: "Keep your mouth shut and your bowels open. Pay as you go, or don't go." Older people often get away with stuff like that.

Many common clichés and ancient proverbs condense great truth into simple equations. Only a very few ever contain such brilliance and brevity on matters of universal importance. It's the kind of thing we expect only from geniuses and small children. And from God.

Wouldn't it be nice if we had a single formula to resolve every interpersonal problem we could ever expect to encounter? Something that always yielded the best results? Something like, "In everything... treat people the same way you want them to treat you" (Matthew 7:12) Something you could understand today, but work out in the real world for the rest of your life. The person who came up with that one would be worth listening to.

He also came up with these:

"But seek first His kingdom and His righteousness; and all these things shall be added to you."

(Matthew 6:33)

"Not everyone who says to Me 'Lord, Lord', will enter the kingdom of heaven; but he who does the will of My Father who is in heaven."

(Matthew 7:21)

"For whoever wishes to save his life will lose it; but whoever loses his life for My sake shall find it."

(Matthew 16:25)

"I am the way, and the truth, and the life; no one comes to the Father but through me."

(John 14:6)

As we unlock the secrets of the world in which we live, we find a most unexpected phenomenon: "On the other side of complexity, lies simplicity." After all is said and done, the answer often comes down to surprising magnificently beautiful explanations of reality. That's why theoretical physicists are all running pell-mell in search of a single complete theory of everything.

We have an appetite for simple answers even though we know that we live in a very complex world. If we search far enough our appetite is appeased. We find simple complexity.

Another old man condensed a lifetime of experience into a few words. He was the only one of the followers of Jesus of Nazareth, the crucified rabbi, who lived to old age. He was also one of his closest friends. After watching the struggling church emerge during the middle half of the first century, John summarized for them the essence of what he understood.

In a short letter to friends around A.D. 90 or so, he wrote the following:

"Beloved, let us love one another, for love is from God; and everyone who loves is born of God and knows God. The one who does not love does not know God, for God is love." (1 John 4:7,8)

So, we see from this that our defining characteristic is to be love from God.

"By this the love of God was manifested in us, that God has sent His only begotten Son into the world so that we might live through Him." (1 John 4:9)

And this is how God's love becomes our source of love.

"In this is love, not that we loved God, but that He loved us and sent His Son to be the propitiation for our sins." (1 John 4:10)

This is God's love toward us.

"Beloved, if God so loved us, we also ought to love one another." (1 John 4:11)

And this is its result.

"No one has beheld God at any time; if we love one another, God abides in us, and His love is perfected in us." (1 John 4:12)

God's perfect love will be seen in and through us, as we love one another.

"By this we know that we abide in Him and He in us, because He has given us of His Spirit."

"And we have beheld and bear witness that the Father

has sent the Son to be the Savior of the world."

"Whoever confesses that Jesus is the Son of God, God abides in him, and he in God." (1 John 4:13-15)

Our knowledge, our witness, and our confession are all contained within love.

"And we have come to know and have believed the love which God has for us. God is love, and the one who abides in love abides in God, and God abides in him." (1 John 4:16)

As we live in love, God lives in us.

"By this, love is perfected with us, that we may have confidence in the Day of Judgment; because as He is, so also are we in this world." (1 John 4:17)

The result is that our confidence is completely in His love.

"There is no fear in love; but perfect love casts out fear, because fear involves punishment, and the one who fears is not perfected in love. We love, because He first loved us." (1 John 4:18,19)

Because He has loved us, we are never afraid to love. And we don't love out of fear.

"If someone says, 'I love God,' and hates his brother, he is a liar; for the one who does not love his brother whom he has seen, cannot love God whom he has not seen." (1 John 4:20)

Love is not merely our words—it has become our identity.

"And this commandment we have from Him, that the one who loves God should love his brother also." (1 John 4:21)

Just one simple, upside down, counterintuitive, and superhuman trick.

11

Sky Gods

Life in Another Dimension Right Now

"For though we walk in the flesh, we do not war according to the flesh." (2 Corinthians 10:3)

In the early days of aviation, when men first began to hunt and kill each other in the sky, they operated their flying machines in three dimensions of space. In their minds though, they continued to think as if they were still confined to the surface of the earth. Though mankind had entered the heavens, they fought and died like earthbound mortals who only dreamt of flight. It would be decades before they fully realized what they now possessed. When they finally did awake, the realization transformed the battle.

On the ground, two-dimensional speed and maneuverability were the essential components of war. If you could outrun or out-turn the opponent, you could prevail. Initially, it was no different in the air. Success went to the airplane with the most powerful engine or the most agile wing design. The advantage of terrain or reinforcements was lost in the open sky. Pilots relied on surprise and luck until they gained enough experience to know when to turn tail and run or when to stay and fight. It all came down to very simple physics and the ability to press any advantage to victory.

In this environment of equals, a chosen few seemed to possess mystical skill at the controls of a flying machine. It didn't matter who had the upper hand to begin with. In the end, they won. They were called "aces." They thought differently and saw what no one else could see. They saw what no one else could even imagine. They would invent the most unorthodox, unexpected, even counterintuitive, three-dimensional maneuvers in order to win—and they always won.

These men knew when to engage and they knew when to wait. The machines they flew performed miracles to the amazement of comrades and the short-lived dismay of their enemies. They couldn't always explain how they did it, but they could always show you.

Flying on the wing of an ace was a good way to stay alive. It was also a good way to become an ace yourself. The ace was no mere mortal. They were the sky gods.

An element of air combat maneuvers had yet to be uncovered for many years. In effect, the early aces had tapped into something powerful that they did not completely understand. They understood *that* it worked but they didn't really know *why*.

As men began to comprehend this new world, they became free to explore ideas and develop tactics. They began to take full advantage of three dimensions and the resulting exchange of kinetic and potential energy. Energy management and energy maneuvering became the window into a new world of better airplane design and greater achievement in air superiority.

As man learned to conform to the laws of aerodynamics and exploit the laws of physics that governed this new dimension, he also began to succeed in this realm. The impossible became possible and the unthinkable became routine. Mankind began as an earthbound creature, with all the thoughts and limitations inherent to a wingless being. He became a flying creature with a new perspective, and new abilities, and a vision and appetite for more.

What men had only dreamed of since before the days of Icarrus, was unleashed. Every detail of every airplane is now designed to take advantage of this boundless place that was once so unnatural to man. It now seems as if mankind was meant for this all along. The rulers of the earth have become the rulers of the sky.

And there are other new dimensions that await our discovery and embrace.

The dimension of the Spirit is a higher realm of exploration and the "law of the Spirit of Life in Christ Jesus" (Romans 8:2) is the way of entry. While spiritual aces have been around for millennia, the "mystery which has been hidden from the past ages" (Colossians 1:26) has been made known to all who know Jesus Christ.

It is belief in Him as the One and Only Son of God that results in faith. This faith is expressed in a life of obedience to Him in love, resulting in a righteousness not derived from the Law but from faith. "Without faith, it is impossible to please Him," (Hebrews 11:6).

So, believers follow Jesus into this life of the Spirit and have a new paradigm for living while simultaneously remaining right where they are. In fact, the apostle Paul writes, "the life which I now live in the flesh, I live by faith in the Son of God, who loved me, and delivered Himself up for me" (Galatians 2:20). Life in the flesh becomes life by the Spirit. This new way of living, through Jesus Christ, is also our entrance into eternity. Peter writes, "for in this way the entrance into the eternal kingdom of our Lord and Savior Jesus Christ will be abundantly supplied to you." (2 Peter 1:11) Paul writes to the Corinthians, "The first man, Adam, became a living soul. The last Adam (Jesus Christ) became a life-giving spirit." (1 Corinthians 15:45)

Living our physical lives here and now, while participating in the spiritual kingdom of heaven and its activities and purposes, is only accomplished as we become more adept at life in another dimension. They overlap and intermingle, and Christ-followers maneuver in both dimensions.

This spiritual life is sustained by the Word of God. "Man does not live by bread alone but man lives by everything that proceeds from the mouth of the Lord" (Deuteronomy 8:3). Because God's revealed Word, the Scripture, is the unlimited source of "teaching, reproof, correction, and training in righteousness" (2 Timothy 3:16), the Life of the Spirit will flourish as we willingly align ourselves with His Word.

Like a pilot who enters the heavens and becomes a creature of the sky, the Christian enters into the kingdom of the heavens and becomes a creature of that place. Like the pilot who learns to amaze and soar above the world with grace and ease, so the believer learns to become free from the constraints of the flesh to live a stunning and "unnatural" life that is pleasing to God. He is free to explore this remarkable realm and become more like the Savior and Lord who made it accessible.

Even so, there is a guiding principle that rules this new place. Just as the laws of aerodynamics must be embraced to excel in flight, so the law of love is the defining characteristic of the Spirit. It is a law because the nature of the Spirit requires love. It is still a free choice, however, because the very nature of love requires that one choose it.

The United States of America is a country originally built on a foundation of principles and ideals. The rule of law and the pursuit of liberty have guided America to a remarkable place that civilization has never before seen. With all of its shortcomings and failures, it is still a place where a human being can embrace the rule of law and the liberty of individuals, and be transformed by the experience.

Imagine then, what kind of a place would be in store for humankind if we all embraced the rule of love. To what heights might we soar in such a place? What new worlds might we discover? How might we be transformed?

When every detail of every life is so arranged as to take advantage of this boundless place, for now so unnatural to man, we might find that we were meant for it all along.

12

Love Love

Like a Moth, Be Drawn to the Flame

"Knowledge makes arrogant, but love edifies."
(1 Corinthians 8:1)

It is said there is a danger of loving love rather than loving God. We should never replace love for Jesus Christ with a love for love itself. I am inclined to believe that such words are somewhat misguided because they sell love short. In fact, what may appear to be a love for love cannot be. The definition of love won't allow it.

For example, a love of doing good deeds is not a love for love, because good deeds can be done without love. A love of the satisfaction felt in loving is not a love for love, because satisfaction is not love. The same is true for loving the ideal of love, or the hope of love, or the pursuit of love, and any others. They are not love of love but love of something else.

To love love is *to* love. There is no danger in that. God is love. Jesus said that to love God, and your neighbor as yourself, fulfills the law. To love love, is to love the essence of God Himself. To love is to become like Him and His Only Son, Jesus Christ. Imitation is always the sincerest form of flattery—or worship. Who could believe that to pursue such a life somehow diminishes devotion to God?

If love is our highest practical goal, then perhaps from that lofty vantage point we may at least glimpse our destiny. To love may not be the treasure, but it most certainly will lead us to it. To love love is to be the moth enchanted by the light and so drawn into the flame.

Love. I can accept the goodness of the concept. I can recognize how essential it is to a worthwhile life. I can even acknowledge the imperative placed upon me by its nature and demand. I can clearly imagine its result.

So I choose to love.

Then I go out to an indifferent and even hostile world. I encounter obstructions blocking my will and I experience revulsion to my sensibilities. I see myself, through much effort at times, doing loving things and trying to love. But I find that I really don't love. I find that I can act loving and, at the same time, not even like the object of my action. The person I should love, the one for whom I am doing these loving things, I can even despise. This hypocrisy can't be love. If it's not, then I can't love as I should. Especially in the face of contempt, hatred, indifference, or just plain obnoxious stupidity.

Oh, I can love when it's easy. I can love when I am loved in return. Anybody can. But I cannot love as love demands that I should. I am too selfish, self-centered, self-absorbed, and self-interested to love. I would have never realized this fact unless I had resolved to try to love. That's when I discovered that I could not.

I must be convicted of my need for love before it can ever become a part of me. When I try to love, I am led to the truth about myself (that I cannot) and to my need for repentance. So I repent.

I find myself truly unhappy with the fact that love is not easy for me. I admire love. I aspire to love. I desire to love as God loves, as Jesus Christ loves, but for now it's beyond me. My heart is just not in it. This truth makes my heart feel like a stone. I want a new heart. I want a heart of flesh, not of stone. I want a heart that beats for the good of others—a heart that can truly love.

God is the only one who can give me that heart. When I have turned from self, He is there. When I am ready, God pours His love into me. He forgives me of my selfishness and pride. He forgives me for my lack of concern for others. He forgives me for my arrogance, my ignorance, and my insolence. He who is forgiven much can love much.

So I choose to love.

Love comes easier to me now but that doesn't mean that it's easy. I'm always ready to regress. Going back to my old ways takes no effort. Like lions on a fresh kill, my old self and it's desires and habits attack at every opportunity. But I don't want to be unloving anymore. My heart is becoming different.

So I choose to love.

I'm faced with the challenge of people who don't get it. Loving doesn't come any more naturally to them than it comes to me. I still want to convince them of how much God loves them. I still want them to know what kind of life they could have with Jesus Christ. I want them to see how great life can be in spite of circumstances. But their minds are focused elsewhere. They don't seem to care or even notice. They seem blind to such light and hope. It's almost as if they love the darkness. I can't get through. Conflicts arise. There's often no resolution.

So I choose to love.

People around me are always lashing out. The world is a vicious place for many who have been injured by it. If they can, they protect themselves. When they can no longer defend themselves, they give up like an exhausted fighter who lowers his head and just absorbs blow after blow. I don't know how it comes to this. Sometimes I don't know what to say or how to make it right. The abusers and the abused even share a common misery. Unhappiness and despair are close cousins of rage and contempt.

My role is uncertain, so I choose to love.

Arguments arise over ideas and values. The heart chooses its treasure and the mind defends it to the bitter end. The defenses are solid, the heart secure. The mind will die on the battlefield before it ever surrenders what the heart has chosen. The mind is but an obedient soldier defending the fortress of the heart. But there is a secret door that even the mind cannot defend; it is a door that is locked from within and the heart has the only key. A free will, given to the heart by God Himself, is the master of the castle and can never be coerced. A free will, however, can always respond to love.

Love can outmaneuver and overcome. Love can defeat the defenses of the mind. Love can penetrate the fortress and take the heart willingly captive. Love can be invited in and given the place of honor in the heart and the mind will have no choice but to defend the castle against all others. So the heart must be guarded closely; it is the wellspring of life. And so I choose to love.

Ideas are important. Doctrine and theology will always have their place. Programs, rules, and systems are useful. But love alone can completely transform both the lover and the loved.

I choose to love.

13

Christian Countermeasures

Special Operations behind Enemy Lines

"The whole world lies in the power of the evil one."
(1 John 5:19)

The Army Ranger sat comfortably in front of the snapping fire. His casual demeanor and quiet confidence masked an intensity and determination forged during five deployments to war. Hundreds of successful missions into enemy strongholds under the cover of darkness had confirmed for him the value of his training. "Frank the Tim" knew what he was made of and how to execute his assignment wherever the "Operations Order" indicated. Only twenty-three years old, yet without the carelessness of inexperience so common to youth, he came to talk about following Jesus Christ through the eyes of a Spec-Ops Warrior. Through his eyes.

"Everything about my training as a soldier has a parallel in my Christian life," he claimed, setting the context for the interview. "Basic Training is where you learn respect and discipline. It's the foundation you build on. You have to get it first or you have no foundation. You have to learn to respect God."

"Advanced Individual Training is next. A.I.T. is a chance to develop certain skills and to train in a specialty. For some people that's all it means to be a Christian—be disciplined and develop your gift or talent. Then they go out and try to spread the gospel and do some good. I think there's more to it than that."

"For me the next step was Airborne School. It was literally a leap of faith. That's where I had to say 'my life is no longer in my own hands. I'm willing to do whatever it takes to accomplish the mission.' Until you trust God with your life and agree to carry out His orders no matter how you feel, you haven't become very useful to Him."

I was drawn in by his matter-of-fact approach to the subject. He didn't seem to notice that there were other points of view to be considered. He was a warrior talking about the realities of war. On this subject, he was the expert and I was the student. I asked him to discuss the importance of training.

"Everything is training, because everything you do affects how you react in a critical situation. From the time you get out of bed in the morning until you lay down at night."

At first I wasn't sure whether he was talking about war or the Christian life. Soon I realized he was talking about both.

"So what if a Christian doesn't believe they're really in a war?" I asked.

"How can anyone believe that we're not in a war? All you have to do is look around and see what's going on in the world. There are battles being fought everywhere. Life is a battle"

"But what would happen if someone forgets they're in a battle?" I wondered aloud.

"People die." he answered as quickly as my words

crossed the space between us. "You can *never* forget that you are in a war. That's when bad things happen. The enemy doesn't forget."

We talked about the fear of death and how it can limit a soldier's effectiveness. We discussed dealing with the wounded and how "You never leave anyone behind. *Never.*" He described how everyone has different jobs and skills and how they all work together to accomplish the mission. He told me of those who's job it is to get the wounded off the battlefield and to those who can care for them until they're better.

I listened as he spoke of his command structure in the Army and of the God who commands his life. We talked together for over three hours and covered every conceivable connection. He moved so seamlessly between his life as a soldier and his life as a Christ follower that any dividing lines became blurred. Then I realized that there were no lines for him.

It wasn't until he spoke about his mission as a warrior that I began to understand the depth of this metaphor for every Christian. It wasn't until then that I stopped thinking of it as a metaphor at all. We *are* at war. But it's a different kind of war and the weapons are different too.

The apostle Paul writes this to the church in Corinth. "For though we walk in the flesh, we do not war according to the flesh, for the weapons of our warfare are not of the flesh, but divinely powerful for the destruction of fortresses." (2 Corinthians 10:3,4)

He writes to the church in Rome, "Do not be overcome by evil, but overcome evil with good." (Romans 12:21)

Our current situation is that the whole world is on a path to destruction from which God provides an escape because of His great love for all of humankind. He forgives all who will turn back to Him and does so through the sacrifice of His Only Son, Jesus Christ. As Christ followers, we are called to make that message clear to the world as ambassadors for Christ. But even so, there is an enemy as old as time who would rather we all die.

We are behind enemy lines in this world and to pretend otherwise is not only blind, but also foolish. The war is obvious enough to anyone who cares to be honest.

The question left is this: how do we make the message clear? Our rationalistic culture has many of us convinced that the path to salvation is right through the middle of the human brain. That idea is syncretism of the most obvious kind. Since knowing truth involves the whole person, we will never merely educate ourselves into eternity. We have taken the church and given it the mission of a school when it's real mission is to demonstrate the love of God to the world. God's love is what transforms a person. The school is a supporting institution.

There are more than enough opportunities to live what our faith proclaims. This world is a target-rich environment for anyone bent on combating the effects of sin whether suffered or inflicted. Storming the gates of hell with the sacrificial love of God starts right out the front gate of our own yard or even inside that gate—within our homes. Heaven waits again for the church to step bravely out of the schoolhouse and into the battle.

It's time for we Christians to figure out something that the rest of the world has been telling us all along.

"If I speak with the tongues of men and of angels, but do not have love, I have become a noisy gong or a clanging cymbal. If I have the gift of prophecy, and know all mysteries and all knowledge; and if I have all faith, so as to remove mountains, but do not have love, I am nothing."

(1 Corinthians 13:1-3)

I asked my warrior friend to explain the fundamentals of how to defeat an enemy. This is what he said: "You go in undetected. You use overwhelming force of numbers. You do your job exactly the way you trained and go to the center and strike with speed and the element of surprise. You go right to the heart. If you can take out the center, the enemy crumbles."

Unwarranted, not obligated, and unexpected sacrificial love in response to evil and any of its devastating effects, always enjoys the element of surprise. It is the ultimate Christian countermeasure to the enemy's worst assault. Love alone strikes to the center of the heart. It is truly the most effective apologetic and its pursuit is the finest curriculum for Christian growth. It is in fact the message, the means, and the strategy of God.

There are now Christians everywhere who are willing to penetrate the enemy's strongholds with the love of God at every opportunity and at any cost. In the wake of disaster and devastation or in the face of rejection and ridicule they are "salt" and "light". They are the "One-Trick Ponies" who see clearly that they have been called to carry on the work that Jesus began of proclaiming and demonstrating God's astonishing, extravagant, life-changing love in a broken and hostile world.

God's coordinated offensive has begun with a Special Forces assault. It will end with an invasion. And all of creation is on edge—awaiting the outcome—of God's simple plan to save the world.